JESUS,
B.C.

JESUS, B.C.

GERALD MANN

Riverbend
Press

Austin, Texas 78746

Published by: Riverbend Press, Austin, Texas

Library of Congress
Catalog Card Number (*Applied For*)
ISBN 0-9647272-7-7

10 9 8 7 6 5 4 3 2 1

Printed in the United States of America

For
Jessica, Garrett, Carder,
and Sasha—
My Salt and Light

Table of Contents

Other Books by Gerald Mann:

- The Book of Wisecracks
- Common Sense Religion
- When the Bad Times Are Over for Good
- When One Day at a Time Is Too Long

From
the Author...

Almost twenty years ago I wrote a book on Jesus' Sermon on the Mount, which was published under the title, *Why Does Jesus Make Me Nervous?*

The project was a compromise on my part. I wanted another title and a different approach.

It came down to a standoff between me and the publisher. Either I had to change the title and revise the manuscript for the prescribed audience, or go elsewhere. I relented due to time constraints and the desire to be published.

To the publisher's credit, the book achieved its goals. Yet, I have always wanted to see the unabridged version in print.

Also, I have a much clearer vision of what I was trying to say in those days.

I foresaw the recurrence of the search for the historical Jesus behind the *Christ of faith*. The information age (also known as the *post-Christian* or the *postmodern*) would force believers to reexamine the historical roots of Christianity and search for ways to restate the Good News of Jesus, the Christ, in more cosmopolitan terms. The world was about to be downsized to a global village where Christians would be outnumbered.

I felt then, as I do now, that our best hope was to recast the timeless themes of our faith into a more user-friendly vernacular.

I am grateful, these two decades later, to have a second opportunity.

Gerald Mann

CHAPTER ONE:
Jesus,
B. C.

Jesus, B. C.

The title of this book is not a play on words. *Jesus, B.C.* refers to Jesus *before* Christianity. It refers to his life and teachings before they were dogmatized, ritualized, moralized, and institutionalized into a religion called *Christianity*.

I do not think Jesus intended to found another religion. The world already had plenty. He came to demonstrate a way of loving God, each other, and ourselves which includes and transcends the finest in all religion. His mission was to make humans whole, finished, perfected—*saved*.

He called his effort *the way*. His first disciples called themselves *followers of the way*. They were not yet *Christians*. That would come later when outside observers gave them the label (Acts 11:26).

Christianity is what we've done to *the way*.

It was unavoidable. We must have a container in which to carry our faith experience. But we tend to end up worshipping the container instead of the contents. Whenever this happens, we must attempt to dig down through the layers of tradition and hear **Jesus, B.C.**

That is my aim here—to let the Sermon on the Mount speak to us in the first person, and to take it *seriously*.

X-rated

When they first began rating movies, someone made a tongue-in-cheek suggestion that ministers rate their sermons accordingly. That way, the listeners would be forewarned.

G-rated sermons would mean "generally acceptable to everyone." They would be filled with cream-of-wheat platitudes like, "Go ye and smile." G-sermons should elicit responses like *wonderful, warm, marvelous*.

M-rated sermons would be for more mature audiences. Filled with flowery vocabulary and heavy on scholarly quotations, M-sermons make mild suggestions to change, but reserve qualifiers which allow the minister to retreat if he's challenged.

R-rated sermons are restricted to those willing to submit themselves to God for correction. No esoteric jargon here! R-sermons indicate that the preacher has an outside source of income, and they are called *controversial*.

X-rated sermons are usually preached only once. They're the kind that gets prophets killed. Bags should be packed and insurance premiums paid before preaching X-sermons. Most important, the X-rated sermon is always labeled *unchristian*, because it completely shatters preconceived notions of religion.

The Sermon on the Mount is an X-rated sermon! Throughout history, the church hasn't known quite what to do with it.

The early church took it seriously, until the cause spread to the Gentile world. Afterward, its teachings were thought to apply only to monastics who were secluded from the real world.

Until the Renaissance and Reformation ushered in literacy on a wider scale, the Sermon on the

Mount lay dormant. When it was resurrected, the reformers either made it into a new legalism or saw it as an unattainable ethic meant to drive us to plead for mercy. As they saw it, Jesus never intended for mere mortals to practice his instructions. From their point of view, he was setting ideals so high that we humans are forever forced to remain humble.

In the early twentieth century, Albert Schweitzer and others concluded that Jesus was a deluded apocalyptic rabbi who thought the end of the world was imminent. The Sermon on the Mount prescribed emergency measures as the End approached. No one should be expected to take Jesus' words literally. They cannot be applied to modern sociopolitical realities. For example, how could we *not* resist our enemies if they were Hitler or the KKK? Or how could we give to everyone who begs?

Neorthodox thinkers altered this view of the Sermon. Jesus was not delusional, but he did set moral standards in the Sermon which can never be reached in this broken world. We should constantly *strive* for Jesus' ideals; but we should realize that we cannot reach them. The best we can hope to reach is *justice*. The ideal is *agape love,* and only Jesus ever attained this ideal.

We should never grow complacent or satisfied with justice. We should always reach for the ideal, but accommodate it to reality.

The Sermon on the Mount sets forth principles, not laws.

These principles should judge us and remind us that the best we can attain in some cases is the *lesser* of *evils*. For example, war is evil; but so is Hitler. The ideal is that we love Hitler and turn the other cheek. But if we do, Hitler will kill millions more. So, a war to stop Hitler is the *better* of two *bad* choices.

Situation ethics took the Sermon on the Mount a step further. Rather than moral absolutes, its teachings are applied only to the situation in which Jesus found himself when he spoke. They relate to us today *only as they are applicable*.

Futurists claim that the Sermon's commands are for some future, glorious time when God establishes utopia on earth. In other words, Jesus was giving us a preview of life in the Kingdom to come.

My point in all of the above is not to give you a history lesson, but to illustrate how difficult it has been for believers through the ages to take the Sermon on the Mount seriously.

Every effort to put the Sermon into practice has ended with an accommodation.

Otto Reithmueller understood this when he said of the Sermon:

> Like a magnetic mountain, it has attracted the greatest spirits with undiminished force through all the centuries. For that reason also, it has had to put up with more opposition, distortion, dilution, and emasculation than any other writing in the literature of the world.[1]

Ghandi supposedly remarked that he would gladly become a Christian if Christians would only follow the teachings of Jesus in the Sermon on the Mount.

Prejudices: Yours and Mine

We cannot escape our culture and history entirely. Someone has said that when we think we are thinking we are only rearranging our prejudices.

[1] Otto Riethmueller, "The City and the Mount," **The Student World** 30 (1937):203

There are several prejudices I hold toward the Sermon on the Mount which I recognize, and am willing to name up front.

First,

I lean toward the view that Jesus was *not* issuing a new set of rules, but a set of *high principles* aimed at making us stretch and never be satisfied with our goodness. Indeed, there *are* rare occasions where the rules don't apply; but living up to the *principles* in the Sermon on the Mount *always should be our goal.*

Second,

the Sermon was for disciples only—for those who had already signed on. Both Matthew and Luke indicate that the growing crowds prompted Jesus to draw aside his disciples and teach them. Things were getting out of hand; his celebrity status was overshadowing his mission.

The disciples needed to know what it meant to follow him in everyday life. He was not primarily a *miracle worker*, he was a **revealer**. He had come to show people what God was really like and what God intended for all people to become—namely, like him! And he had come to die in order to make this possible.

The commands in the Sermon are
not rules for earning God's favor.
They are the results of experienc-
ing God's favor. They are for
people who have already met God
in Jesus.

Third,

the Sermon is not a full-blown theology of Jesus. It
does not contain *all* that he taught. For example,
the Great Commandment—Love God with all your
might and your neighbor as yourself—is not mentioned, or the meaning of his death and resurrection, or the work of the Holy Spirit, or the Church.

Fourth,

the Sermon is not a once-delivered address. It is a
collection of the sayings and teachings of Jesus given
at various times and later organized by Matthew or
one of his disciples. This is supported by the fact
that Luke's rendition of the Sermon is much shorter.

Fifth,

the Sermon cannot be understood apart from Jesus' concept of the *Kingdom of God* or the *Kingdom of Heaven*. Both are synonymous in my view.

What is meant by the phrase, *Kingdom of God?* In simplest terms, it means wherever God's will is King, or wherever he reigns—wherever he is sovereign. The Kingdom of God refers to God's sovereignty over any person or community that acknowledges him as King.

The Bible speaks of the Kingdom as existing in three stages: *(1) The Kingdom has always existed, because God is the Creator and Lord of all that exists.* But people can reject his lordship because they are free. When they do so, the Kingdom ceases to exist *in them. (2) In Jesus, the Christ, God has brought the Kingdom back into history; therefore, the Kingdom is.* Everyone who accepts Jesus' way has already begun to enter the Kingdom. *(3) However, the Kingdom is also yet to be.* A time is coming when everyone will acknowledge God as King.

In short, the Kingdom that God willed in the creation—which was delayed by our rebellion—has entered the world again in Jesus and is growing to its future consummation.

Finally,

the Sermon on the Mount is the instruction manual for those who choose to be God's partners in bringing in the Kingdom. It is not for wimps. It is for those who want to transform the world.

On his ninety-fifth birthday, Roger Baldwin, founder of the American Civil Liberties Union (ACLU), was asked whether he considered himself a radical. "Yes," he replied, "but not like you mean. I am radical in terms of the Sermon on the Mount...I believe in loving my enemies...I believe the world is one country and that all men are my countrymen."

Whatever we may think of the ACLU, we cannot deny Baldwin's assessment of the Sermon on the Mount. It does indeed call us to make the world one country. It calls us to abandon all of our myths of superiority—our myths of race, creed, clan, and nation—and to submit to God as King.

Summary: The Sermon on the Mount is vintage Jesus, B.C.— before Christianity regionalized and captured him within culture.

It is X-rated in the sense that the church has never dared to take it seriously. Instead of using its commands to change the culture, we have used culture to change the commands.

We must attempt to hear Jesus' words again—unfiltered by centuries of accommodation.

However, we must not make the Sermon more than it is. It doesn't contain all that Jesus taught. It is not a systematic theology; it is a daily instruction manual for living as citizens of the Kingdom that is dawning in the world.

Most of all, we must remember that it is not a new legalism—a way to earn God's favor. It is a *response* to God's favor, which we possess already. We shouldn't expect to be applauded or admired for heeding its instructions. They are for *Kingdom Bringers*.

As Amos Wilder put it years ago:

> *The Sermon on the Mount is directed to those who have begun to enter into the new age and have begun to share its new powers. It should never be forgotten that both its ethical teachings and its confidence in God are spoken in a context of salvation.* [2]

[2] Amos N. Wilder, "The Sermon on the Mount," **The Interpreter's Bible**, 12 vols. (New York: Abingdon Press, 1951)7:160-161

One More Thing:

Do not read further unless you have already read Matthew 5–7 and Luke 6:20-49. You might want to read these texts from several translations. You may discover, as I have, that preexisting *impressions* of what the Sermon says and what it *really* says are two different things.

At any rate, read the Sermon on the Mount, and read it as if *Jesus* were speaking to *you.*

CHAPTER TWO:

The People God Blesses

The People
God Blesses
(Matthew 5:3-12)

Happiness vs. Blessedness

The eight sayings that Jesus uses to introduce the Sermon are not his secret formulas for happiness. I once believed they were. The Greek word, *makarios,* used to introduce the eight sayings, or Beatitudes, can be translated *happy.* That is how I translated it in the first edition of this book.

However, I see now that happiness is too connected to *happenstance* to properly capture the meaning of the word. The traditional word *blessed* is better, because it refers to a state of serenity that remains constant no matter what happens to us.

To be *blessed* means to experience God's own personal affirmation—his *attaboy!* or *attagirl!* It is the experience of hearing God's personal expression of joy.

The *blessing* theme recurs throughout the Bible. When Jesus began his public ministry, he submitted to baptism signifying that he had accepted God's calling. When he emerged from the water, "Heaven was opened to him and he saw the spirit of God descending like a dove and lighting on him. Then he heard a voice from heaven saying: 'Behold, here is my own dear son who gives me great delight!'" (Matthew 3:16-17)

To be *blessed* is to experience God's personal expression of delight or endorsement.

I believe that the desire for *blessing* is our deepest human need. Beneath all of our yearnings is the hunger to be *blessed* by God. When God first called Abraham to be his messenger of redemption, he made a covenant, or contract, with him. Abraham's task was to trust and obey. God's part of the bargain was to *bless* Abraham and make Abraham a *blessing* to his descendants—"I will bless you...so that you will be a blessing" (Genesis 12:2).

When Jesus "sat down and began to teach them" (Matthew 5:2), he knew the deepest question of their heart—*How do we experience God's own personal blessing?* And so, he starts with the exclamation "Oh, how *blessed* are…" Then he proceeds to describe *blessed* people. He doesn't give a lecture or try to define **blessed-ness.** He simply describes eight kinds of people who experience God's blessings and how the blessings are felt.

God Blesses the Poor in Spirit (Matthew 5:3)

Volumes have been written on the meaning of *poor in spirit.* I think the best definition is found in the parable Jesus told about two men who went up to the temple to pray (Luke 18:9). One was a Pharisee, the other a tax collector—two opposites. Pharisees were thought to be the most spiritually rich people on earth. Tax collectors were turncoats who collaborated with Rome to exact taxes from their countrymen for a profit.

The Pharisee in Jesus' story stood apart by himself and proudly thanked God that he was unlike the wicked—"especially like that tax collector over there." He then proceeded to remind God and those nearby of his many spiritual attributes and achievements.

The tax collector couldn't raise his eyes above his navel. Instead of standing apart from others in exclusivistic pride, he stood at a distance in shame. All he could do was beat his breast and mumble, "Mercy—Mercy—Mercy."

Poor in spirit means knowing that we have nothing to brag about when it comes to native goodness. All spiritual merit comes from a merciful God. In and of ourselves, we are beggars when it comes to possessing God's nature (Spirit).

Jesus finishes the parable with an interesting phrase. "I tell you," he says, "the tax collector, not the Pharisee, went home right with God. For everyone who inflates himself will be emptied and everyone who deflates himself will be made great" (Luke 18:14 – my translation).

The words *right with God*, or *justified*, refer to living without barriers between God and us. And being *bonded* with God means partaking of his Kingdom, or living in his neighborhood.

So, the first Beatitude tells us that those who know they are spiritually empty are the ones who experience God's blessing. The Kingdom of Heaven belongs to them—that is, they are always in God's neighborhood—they are *right* with him. They are *in sync.*

In my forty-year journey of faith, whenever I

have experienced the unmistakable presence of God and felt his *blessing*—his personal *attaboy!*—there has been one common element. ***It has always come on the heels of admitting my own spiritual bankruptcy.*** God never places water in my well until I admit that it's dry, and I have no place else to turn. And the *blessing* has always felt like a joyful homecoming—like I am back where I belong.

The *blessed* are the ones who know their spiritual well is dry.

God's neighborhood is theirs.

God Blesses Those Who Mourn (Matthew 5:4)

How could there be a connection between *mourning* and *blessing*? It sounds morbid. Some have said that this second Beatitude is tied to the first—that is, *blessed* are those who mourn their spiritual poverty—those who are sorry for being so unrighteous.

I can't buy this kind of self-disgust. Nowhere did Jesus suggest that self-hatred is a key to blessedness.

I think he's referring to our capacity to care enough to grieve and to be unashamed in displaying it. He's saying people who maintain the capacity to hurt with others and grieve over the brokenness of this world are the ones who hear God's comforting voice. *Blessing* cannot come to those whose hearts have grown too callused to care.

Someone has pointed out that the opposite of love is not hatred, but indifference. Hatred requires that we care enough to feel something.

In the old movie, *The Pawnbroker*, the main character is sitting in his shop looking through his store window. Street thugs are mugging a helpless man. The pawnbroker knows that he cannot stop the mugging, yet he cannot join the ranks of the disinterested. On his desk there is one of those spikes which is used to impale bits of paper.

The pawnbroker slowly places his hand palm-down over the spike and runs the spike all the way through it. It is a grotesque dramatic device often used by Hollywood, but it conveys the truth.

Taking up our cross always precedes *resurrection*. We cannot know real joy unless we share the pain of others. It has been said, "Young men who cannot weep are savages. Old men who cannot laugh are fools."

How is the *blessing* felt by *mourners?* Jesus says, "God himself will comfort them." I didn't know the significance of this statement until the day my son was born. He was two months early, weighed just under two pounds, and had a chest full of fluid. The doctors gave me a grim prognosis. If he survived, he was likely to have brain damage.

I had to be alone. Locking myself in a hospital restroom, I sat in the only place there was to sit, and proceeded to shout obscenities at God. We already had one child with birth defects. This was too much.

After my venting, I was emotionally drained. I sobbed uncontrollably. Finally, I had no more tears.

Just then, an unmistakable voice from within told me, "I have always been your best friend." Then I heard laughter—the laughter of God.

God himself had comforted me—with quiet assurance and with mocking laughter! I was still scared and sad. I mourned, but *not* as one without hope. My son survived and is now a delightful and healthy man. And I know what Jesus meant by the second Beatitude.

God Blesses the Meek
(Matthew 5:5)

Meek is one of those old English words which has changed meanings since the days of King James. Some now translate it as *humble*, but that doesn't quite get it either. First of all, *meek* in no way means weak. It has no hint of passivity.

In ancient Greece, the word was used in the training of animals. During the Peloponnesian wars, for example, a soldier wrote a letter to his betrothed to inform her that he had captured the stallion belonging to an enemy commander. "He is a most splendid animal," the man wrote. "He is faster and stronger than any horse in the field. Yet he responds instantly to the slightest command. He is truly a meek horse!"

So, when Jesus said God blesses the meek, he meant those who allow God to harness and direct their powers—those who channel their strength to its *optimum potential.*

I would say meek means *disciplined,* except the word has become too connected to punishment. In its original sense, disciplined meant *teachable.*

At any rate, Jesus says the *meek* experience God's *blessing.* In what way? "They shall inherit the earth." What does this mean? Is he talking about material benefits here? It is true, after all, that disciplined, teachable people usually end up with the lion's share of the world's best economic and emotional benefits.

However, I don't think Jesus is speaking in materialistic terms here. Some translations read: "They shall receive what God has promised," and say that

Jesus was referring to God's original promise to Abraham. What was that promise? *That Abraham would constantly know God's **blessing** and as a result constantly **bless** others.*

So, Jesus is saying, "Blessed are those who submit their powers to God's direction. They shall experience continuous blessings and be able to bless others."

Nothing in life is more satisfying than *blessing* others. Sam Keene wrote to his aged father to thank him for his life. "Of all the wonderful gifts you gave me," he wrote, "the greatest was your gift of *delight*. You always took delight in us. No matter that we interrupted you, or bothered you. You *lit up* when we walked in."

The reason that blessing others is such a delight is because it means *we* have been blessed. You can't bless if you haven't been blessed! The power to *pass on* the blessing is the greatest power on earth. Truly the *blessers* shall inherit the earth!

God Blesses the Spiritually Starved (Matthew 5:6)

When I was young, I often hunted quail with my father. We'd walk behind the bird dogs for miles. Inevitably, I would get thirsty and hungry at the point farthest from the truck, which Dad had stocked with provisions. When I complained, I always received the same reply. "An Indian," he would say, "always aims straighter on an empty stomach."

The remark became so trite that I grew to detest it. I came to realize that it was his way of telling me to buck up and stop complaining. He would return to the truck on his schedule, not mine.

But, I also remember vividly the taste of those provisions when we did return to the truck. Nowhere else did the water taste as cool and sweet or the tuna fish sandwiches as *gourmet*. And the avocados! We always had one each. They were like the gods' ambrosia!

This is a metaphor for the meaning of the fourth Beatitude. Jesus describes people who are ravenous for *righteousness*, a word that connotes perfect alignment with God's own character. But obviously, they cannot achieve such perfection. They are *too far from the Father's truck*. In fact, they are so far away from God's standards that any talk about doing *better*, or aiming *straighter*, only creates more misery.

These are the ones God blesses. How? By filling them to overflowing. "They shall be filled" means that God will fully *close the distance* between them and him!

This Beatitude is not about the quest for perfection. It's about the *grace* of God! We feel God's love most when we know it is impossible to earn his love. And his grace is proportionate to our acknowledged weakness! The greater our helplessness, the greater his grace!

Jesus doesn't say, "Blessed are those who achieve *perfection*." He says, "Blessed are those who are starving to be like God and know they cannot even come close. They are the ones who finally know God fully."

All of the gods invented before and after Jesus were *cursing* gods. Mortals had to appease them or be cursed. Jesus introduced us to a *blessing* God—a God who blesses us even when we've cursed him! The crucifixion of Jesus was our curse on him. The resurrection of Jesus was his blessing us in return.

Well then, should we try to be good? I mean, if we know we can't, why try? *Because we have to.* It is our nature to attempt moral alignment with God. We are like a tree growing toward light. The good news of this Beatitude is that our hunger, our thirst, is enough.

God Blesses the Merciful (Matthew 5:7)

Someone caught W.C. Fields, an avowed atheist, reading the Bible. His explanation was that he was "looking for loopholes." Many have tried to do likewise with the fifth Beatitude. I certainly have.

There aren't any. *Give* mercy, and you *receive* mercy. *Withhold* mercy, and mercy will be *withheld*. We will speak more of this when we look at Jesus' words on forgiveness later in the Sermon (Matthew 6:14-15).

It is enough here simply to say that there is a *relational law* at work in our lives, and it hinges on mercy. When we give mercy, we place ourselves in *mercy territory*—we place ourselves where mercy is given.

Here's an example. I knew a minister who fed his congregation a steady diet of "hellfire and damnation." He even named sins and sinners from the pulpit. He fashioned himself as a modern prophet, reminding his flock regularly that he was only following God's instructions. He loved them, but he was required to obey God by giving them a weekly "spanking" from his pulpit.

Then he stumbled. It was a minor infraction not worth mentioning here. Immediately, he was pilloried and drummed out of the church. He had created a climate of *no mercy* and he was victimized by his own creation.

Withhold mercy, only if you are not in need of it yourself.

God Blesses the Pure in Heart (Matthew 5:8)

This Beatitude centers in the words, *heart* and *pure*. In Jesus' time, the heart was regarded as the seat of all personality and character. Today we would call it the *subconscious*, or the *mind*. It refers to the seedbed of our drives. Proverbs 23:7 says, "As a man thinks in his heart, so is he."

The word *pure* simply means *clean* in this verse. So, *blessed* are those constantly submitting their motives to God for cleansing.

There are no pure motives, but there are *purified* motives. We cannot escape self-interest. We're sinners, which means we always look out for "Number One." Even a parent who lays down his or her life for a child is declaring that death would be better than life without the child.

But we can refuse to let unexamined motives rule us, and we can redirect our self-interest to a cause beyond our self-gratification.

For example, one of my lifelong demons is a desire for applause. It so happens that I grew up under that curse known as *you coulda' done better, Jerry*. I felt that my every accomplishment was not only a failure, but also an occasion for another lecture.

I caused myself and others much grief until a wise counselor helped me see that this drive for applause was the source of much acting out as well as manipulating for the spotlight.

While I could not restructure my heart—my *engine room*—I could redirect it to a good cause. Of course, I have failed, and will fail again. But when I submit my *engine room* for cleansing, a very curious thing happens. I receive a clearer vision of God. I see him in unexpected places and things.

"The *blessed* are those who do regular *'heart cleaning'*. They shall see God."

God Blesses the Peacemakers (Matthew 5:9)

For years, I had this one wrong! I bought into all of those commentaries about being the *Holy Referee*. I thought Jesus was calling us to a ministry of conflict resolution. After interfering in my share of quarrels, I reexamined the seventh Beatitude.

While he obviously praised peace-negotiators, I think Jesus had more in mind. I think he was talking about making peace within ourselves—about putting a stop to our ongoing battle with God. I think he was talking about the kind of peace-making portrayed in that wonderful movie, *Forest Gump*.

Do you remember Lieutenant Dan? He's the First Lieutenant of Gump's platoon, and his destiny is to die in battle and thus join his several ancestors who have died in every previous war fought by America. A flashback shows Lieutenant Dan in successive wars falling on the battlefield and wearing every uniform from the American Revolution to World War II.

As per his destiny, he is apparently fatally wounded in Viet Nam. Both legs are gone. He is bleeding to death. But this idiot savant, Forest Gump, braves enemy fire and rescues him—winning the Congressional Medal of Honor in the process.

Lieutenant Dan is left with a wheelchair and a "mere Purple Heart." He hates Gump and curses his fate by abusing himself.

Finally, he joins Gump on a shrimp boat which is a joke itself. Then fate smiles. A storm erupts while they're at sea. Lieutenant Dan lashes himself to the mast and dares God to kill him as the lightning flashes and the storm howls.

Miraculously, they survive. The sun reappears. The sea is dead calm. Lieutenant Dan comes down, hoists his stump of a body onto the edge of the boat, and leaps into the water. He swims away and turns toward the camera. We expect him to drown himself.

Instead, a smile covers his face for the first time in years. He whoops with joy and cheers being alive.

Gump's voice-over says something like, "Although Lieutenant Dan never spoke of it, I believe he made his peace with God."

I don't know if the screenwriters and the actors, Tom Hanks and Gary Senise, had the seventh Beatitude in mind when they did that scene, but they visually interpreted it to a tee. For Lieutenant Dan's face revealed that he was seeing God where he never saw him before.

God Blesses the Persecuted (Matthew 5:10-12)

This is where most commentators tell us that we don't know what *real* persecution is. Then they proceed to tell us "tales of gore from days of yore." We learn of martyrs who bravely paid the highest sacrifice for faith. Then we are scolded for not remembering them, and we are reminded of how little we must pay today in order to call ourselves believers.

I'm not mocking this approach. On the contrary, I do feel some shame at how good I have it. And I do wonder if I would have the nerve to pay such a price.

But I must ask myself: How does this Beatitude apply to me? Am I persecuted for doing right and for following Jesus' way?

The truthful answer is that *I* am indeed persecuted for my discipleship. We *all* are. Life and limb may not be in danger, but our reputation, good name, and intention are under attack whenever we dare to share "unorthodox" experiences or viewpoints—whether from the Left or the Right. But the most ominous of my persecutors is my own lower nature. I am attacked by *me*—often and without mercy!

When I decide to forgive, the beast of revenge leaps out of the basement and tells me to nurse my hurts and strike back—or at least to harbor a few morsels of resentment.

When I look at my economic lifestyle and ponder whether I should give *more,* self-pity steps right up and says, "you're already being more generous than most. Don't let guilt and shame get the best of you."

When I'm faced with my aging libido, the voice of fear attacks. "All you need is a young beauty to rejuvenate you. You don't have to abandon your mate. Don't be so American."

I don't believe I ought to go further, except to say that I fear the persecutor *within* far more than any persecutor *outside* of me. In essence, Jesus is saying, "Blessed are you when you are attacked by your *lower* nature for heeding the call of your *higher* nature."

I read this somewhere or I made it up. I don't remember. Anyway, Satan was advising one of his demons on how to corrupt a believer who had decided to place honesty above profit. The junior demon had been making the believer feel regret for reducing his profits.

Satan tells the demon that he must not make the man feel regret. He must make him feel pride. "That way," says Satan, "he will begin to add up how much his belief has cost him. The greater the sum, the greater the pride. And soon he will have the rationalization he needs for setting a limit on his generosity. Pride will insulate him from God's presence. Regret, however, will make him suffer. And whenever a believer suffers, God always comes to stand with him in his time of need."

I am not fearful of the Big Martyr Moment— of being stood before the firing squad because of my faith, or maligned or ridiculed. *I'm fearful of being persecuted by the beasts in my own basement.* But God has an antidote—his personal presence, which I feel as *blessing*.

Summary:

The desire to be blessed by God is the deepest hunger of the human soul. Just as we yearn for parental approval, or "blessing," we yearn to hear God's personal affirmation.

No wonder Jesus opened his "top sermon" by describing eight kinds of people who feel God's blessing.

The poor in spirit are those who know they are spiritually empty. They have nowhere to turn but to God. God's blessing comes to them as a feeling of being *at home* with God—of living in his neighborhood.

God blesses *those who mourn*—those who have the capacity to grieve for the way things are. They will feel the blessing as God's personal comfort in their time of grief.

The meek are those who allow God to harness

their power. They are the teachable giants. They feel God's blessing as the enormous power to bless others.

God blesses *the merciful.* How? By seeing to it that mercy is returned and multiplied.

Those who hunger and thirst to be aligned with God are blessed, because by recognizing that they can never reach their goal, they encounter God's grace. God *fills them up.* He closes the distance between himself and the starving.

Those who "clean-heart" regularly are blessed. By constantly examining their motives and submitting them to God for recycling, they see God in unexpected places.

Blessed are *those who make peace with God.* They shall hear him call them, "my children."

Blessed are *those who are being persecuted by their own lower nature for heeding the call of their higher nature.*

They shall rank with prophets of old.

CHAPTER THREE:
The Way in the World

The Way in the World

(Matthew 5:13-48, 6:22-23)

Why I'm Not a Christian

(Matthew 5:48)

By Jesus' definition in the Sermon on the Mount, I am *not* a Christian. I'll leave it up to you to decide whether you are.

He sums up his revolutionary teachings concerning what his followers are to do in the everyday world by saying, "Be perfect, like your Father in heaven is perfect" (Matthew 5:48).

Before you stop reading, let me add that the tenses of the verbs and the structure of the sentence

should make it read: "Be continuously in the process of becoming like God—who is complete—finished—perfected." The emphasis is on God-like-
ness, which begs the question: What is God like?

Simply put, *God* is like *Jesus*.

In fact, he said, "Since you have seen me, you
have seen the Father" (John 14:9). So a Christian,
by these standards, is someone who has succeeded
in becoming like *Christ*—who was like *God*.

I'm on my way—a **wayfarer**—but I'm not there.
I'm still under construction.

In the second section of the Sermon on the
Mount, Jesus proceeds to describe how wayfarers
are to live for God in the world.

Preserve and Point (Matthew 5:13-16, 6:22-23)

Jesus uses two well-known metaphors to set the
stage for the thunderbolts to come. First, wayfarers are to be like *salt*.

I've heard a flood of lectures on how the word
salt triggered images of flavoring and tastiness in
the minds of those listening to Jesus. The infer-
ence is that believers are supposed to have that spicy

something extra because they know Jesus. Maybe so, but I think the salt metaphor means something else, especially in light of the illustrations that follow. They are demanding and radical.

In those times, salt was used to keep meat from rotting. Its main use was not to flavor food but to preserve the provisions needed for survival.

You are the salt of the earth means *you are to hold society together.* You are to preserve sanity when the world is insane. You are to anchor the ship of civilization against the storm.

Wayfarers march to a different drum. They do not conform. They preserve. They are the glue that keeps things together—the linchpin that keeps the wheels from flying off.

The second metaphor for describing how wayfarers are to live is *light.* Translated, the word *light* was used frequently to refer to a *beacon fire* which guided ships to safe harbor. Wayfarers are to be *way-pointers* to a gracious, loving God. They don't point to themselves; they point to God.

Jesus adds a warning to both metaphors. If salt becomes *neutralized*, it is *worthless*. It cannot stop decay. People can no longer distinguish it from the common dirt they walk on. If a light is not put on a hill to direct others to safe harbor, it is useless. It simply burns energy.

Many scholars believe that Matthew 6:22-23 belongs here. Jesus adds, "If your light points nowhere and illuminates nothing, then it is no different than darkness."

So, wayfarers are to *preserve* and to *point*. No doubt, his listeners wanted to know exactly what being salt and light entailed. They didn't have to wait for long.

The Way and the Law
(Matthew 5:17-20)

There is a difference between being *legal* and being *right*. For example, elected officials of all persuasions frequently defend receiving contributions from certain entities by saying "I did nothing illegal, and I promise I'll never do it again."

At this writing, if public opinion polls are to be

believed, William Clinton's presidency is being jeopardized more by whether he broke a *legal statute* than by whether he had an extramarital sexual affair. If he had an affair, he is in no danger of being impeached. If he broke a law, it is another matter.

Many years ago, the Russian dissident, Alexander Solzhenitsyn, warned Americans not to trade legality for morality. He said he had grown up in a society where there was no legal protection for the individual against the state. It was a barbaric system to be sure, but equally barbaric is the system where everything legal is also right.[1]

This is precisely what Jesus teaches in the Sermon on the Mount. Believers are to obey the law, but they really don't need laws to tell them how to behave. They are to go beyond what is *legally* required.

"Don't think I have come to abolish the Laws of Moses," he says, "I haven't come to abolish them but to take them to a level beyond legality. Anyone who advocates lawlessness will be least in the Kingdom of God. Whoever obeys the Law and teaches others to do so, shall be greatest in the Kingdom of Heaven."

---

[1] Alexander Solzhenitsyn, "The West's Decline in Courage", **Wall Street Journal**, 13 June 1978, p.1.

But then he drives home his point—namely, that keeping legal statutes is child's play compared to what he has in mind. "Unless you are more faithful than the lawyers and Pharisees require, you shall not even make the front door of the Kingdom."

Preserving and *pointing* include being legal, but being legal doesn't mean we are right with God and others. Laws are made to punish and convict and maintain order. They tell us when and what we've done wrong, and what the penalty is for doing so. But they cannot make us *right* with each other or *right* with God. Being legal is necessary, but it is not enough to preserve society and point the way to the Kingdom. Human nature cannot be repaired with additional laws.

Jesus now gives concrete examples of what it means to go beyond legality to morality.

The Way, Beyond Murder (Matthew 5:21-26)

He begins with the most universally punished crime on earth, *murder*. No society can endure if it blinks at homicide, or becomes desensitized toward it.

The Jewish law had very precise rules for defining murder and for punishing it. Jesus goes beyond the overt act of homicide to its root causes.

Refraining from murder is not enough to preserve our common life and to guide it to a higher level. *We must uproot the **seeds** of violence.* He proceeds to list four seeds.

The first seed of violence is *unresolved anger.* "The Law says don't murder. Whoever murders will be judged. But, I say, you will be judged if you nourish your anger into a state of rage." The word *orgitzo* translates as *anger* or *hate*. It refers to all uncontrolled—*orgiastic*—emotions.

The second seed of violence is *name-calling.* When we use derogatory names to label our adversaries, we set up a *we* vs. *they* transaction. We dehumanize people. Once we regard them as aliens— unlike us decent folks—they are *objects*, not persons, and therefore not as worthy to exist as we are.

Apply this to current times. We are obsessed with labeling and dehumanizing. This is especially true during war. We speak of the *enemy* who is a Gook, Chink, Jap, Kraut, etc. ***Name-calling widens the pathway to murder.***

"The Law says, *don't murder*. I say, *don't call your brother 'Raca', or 'Fool'.* If you do, you are paving your own road to hell" (Matthew 5:22).

The third seed of violence is what I call *sanctification of my cause.* It is the universal tendency to enlist God in our disputes against our foes. It's the *Holy War* mentality that has triggered more killing than any other human tendency in history.

Look across the face of our planet and you can name more than one hot spot where opponents have drafted *their* gods to *their* cause: the Middle East, the Balkans, India-Pakistan, Northern Ireland.

Jesus says, "If you go to the altar to make an offering to God, and you remember a dispute with a brother, leave your offering in *front* of the altar— not *on* it—and go make peace with your brother. *Then* come back and make your peace with God" (Matthew 5:23-24).

The fourth seed of violence is what I call the *court-as-a-first-resort mentality.* Instead of going through the difficulty of solving conflicts on a personal basis, we leave it to a third party—a *judge.* Once we abandon personal responsibility in reconciliation, we lose control of the outcome. Our foe ceases to be a person and becomes a plaintiff or a defendant.

We lose all *personal* communications and relationships. The decision is irrevocable. We may receive material satisfaction, but the enmity never goes away.

Murder is a crime. No dispute
here. But it is the symptom of four
moral crimes of the heart, namely:
(1)unresolved anger;
(2)derogatory labeling which turns
our foes into objects;
3)giving "holy" sanction to our
side, which enables us to justify
the worst; and
(4) abdicating personal responsibility for reconciliation to an im-
personal third party.

Jesus tackled symptoms. If we are to *preserve* and *point*, we must do likewise.

The Way, Beyond Adultery (Matthew 5:27-30)

When Jesus used the word *adultery*, his listeners had no problem understanding what he meant.

Adultery meant sex outside of marriage, period! It referred to premarital sexual intercourse and extramarital sexual intercourse of the physical kind.

In this, he was merely echoing the laws of Moses and the Prophets. The Bible places adultery alongside murder when it comes to the actions that break down a civilization. It is strictly forbidden.

However, Jesus again points to a higher level for wayfarers. "The Law says *no adultery*. I say *no lust!* Anyone who looks at a woman and wants to possess her is guilty of committing adultery with her in his heart."

And, as if that weren't strict enough, he fires another volley. "If your eye causes you to sin, *gouge it out!* If your hand causes you to sin, *cut it off!*"

What are we to make of this? Does more than a handful of people on our planet take these words seriously anymore?

Shouldn't we place this in historical context? There were no birth control methods in those days. This was *pre-pill*. People were married off at puberty. Women were property. Extramarital sex *spoiled the property*.

In short, shouldn't we realize that biblical sexual morés were primitive rules applicable to a primitive society? After all, we have accommodated passages from Leviticus, which make *homosexualism*, *adultery*, and even *disobedience to parents* into *capital crimes*. And haven't we done likewise with St. Paul's admonition that slaves "stay in their place?"

I am the first to admit that biblical ethics should and must be reinterpreted within a modern context. But I am not so anxious to blink at Jesus' words about adultery.

All discussion about sexual right and wrong must begin and end with the question: *Am I in charge of my sex drive, or is it in charge of me?*

Our sexual mores reveal our view of human nature. Are we creatures of conditioned response or can we control our moral decisions? If you are a psycho-determinist, then you regard sexual restraint as damaging. If you believe in self-determination, then sexual restraint is a tool for cementing relationships and stabilizing society.

I am well aware that if we reserved church membership only for those who were virgins on their wedding nights, and those who never had an affair afterwards, we would have an empty church or a church full of liars.

But why should this make Jesus' words any less true? We are in no hurry to disregard what he says about anger or charity. Why should we hurry to ignore what he says about sexual behavior?

In 1934, J. D. Unwin published his book, *Sex and Culture,* after examining the sexual morés of eighty-six different societies. He was trying to verify Freud's notion that civilization is a by-product of repressed sexuality. He had no religious or moral agenda.

He discovered a direct correlation between a society's sexual restraint and its "expansive energy." Whenever monogamy and chastity were prevalent values, the society expanded. Whenever the society was sexually promiscuous, it receded; its creativity and productivity waned. His conclusion was that every society must choose between sexual restraint and growth, or promiscuity and decline.

When I wrote of this twenty years ago, America seemed to be in decline. The cold war was at its peak and Japanese productivity was outstripping America's.

Now, at the turn of the century, I wonder if Unwin's thesis still holds. America is the world's superpower economically and militarily. The crime rate is down. Employment is at an all time high. On the surface, Unwin would appear incorrect.

But consider this. America took a big turn to the right in the 1980's, politically and spiritually. In 1974, there were only twenty-four churches in America with an average Sunday attendance of 2,000 or more. Now there are twenty times that many and the numbers are multiplying exponentially.

A great spiritual awakening is taking place almost unnoticed by the media. A case can be made that Americans are finally outgrowing the so-called lawless sixties. We may outlive the hippies yet, or discover that most of them were not as promiscuous as first reported.

On the other hand, America may be in more trouble than it appears. The world has shrunk. Manufacturing and agriculture are going abroad. Our educational system may not provide the resources needed for us to maintain superiority in the information age. American culture could be in the cut-flower stage of its life.

At any rate, Jesus and history are yet to be disproved regarding sexual restraint and societal health. Sexuality is a powerful force which must be harnessed or left to rule us. That is why Jesus uses the dramatic metaphors of gouging out our eyes and chopping off our hands.

Sex is not a drive to be treated casually. Give into it and it consumes you. Manage it and it becomes a great gift. And management begins on the "inside." Our most effective sex organ is the mind. Our sexual behavior germinates there, and there is where we are to deal with it.

Whatever we may think of Jesus' words about "looking on a woman with lust," we cannot deny that adultery is first and foremost an *inside job*. It begins the moment we view another person as something to possess—as an object to use. Gratifying oneself by exploiting another, adulterates—*pollutes*—relationships. Society cannot survive the *thingification* of persons.

The Way, Beyond Divorce (Matthew 5:31-32)

It is as difficult these days to listen to Jesus' words about *divorce* as to his words about adultery.

Depending on whose numbers you accept, the divorce rate ranges from severe to epidemic. The casualizing of marriage correlates with the casualizing of extramarital sex.

When Jesus spoke, marriages were arranged and divorce was strictly a male issue. Men could "put away their wives" but not vice versa. In fact, the only legal protection for the wife was a *certificate of divorcement* that declared her to be no longer the property of her husband.

There were two conflicting schools of thought regarding when and how a man could discard his wife. The strict view forbade divorce except in cases where wives committed adultery or proved not to be virgins on their wedding day. The liberal view permitted divorce for just about any reason the husband wished.

Jesus cut neither party any slack. As **salt** and **light**, wayfarers were to keep their wedding vows. The *adultery "exception"* is not present in many early biblical manuscripts. Scholars see it as a "late edition" to the original text, or they interpret Jesus' words as follows: "If a man divorces his wife *even though she has not committed adultery,* then he makes her commit adultery if she marries again" (Matthew 5:32).

The center of biblical religion is the covenant

of faithfulness between God and people. Marriage is a reflection of this God-people covenant. The covenant relationship between God and people cannot survive without a covenant relationship between people and people.

Jesus was not being legalistic in forbidding divorce. He was being *personalistic*. Human society cannot survive without family solidarity. Divorce should never be viewed as an option for wayfarers!

Well then, are all divorced persons doomed? Of course not. They are no more doomed than those who *lust in their hearts, or nourish their anger*, or *feed their pride*.

Jesus is not trying to exclude a *particular* kind of sinner from the fold, nor should we. He is simply stating the obvious. People who make marriage casual, and court easy divorce, are not being *salt* or *light*.

Can divorced persons remarry and remain within the grace of God? Of course! Anyone who thinks otherwise should read carefully Jesus' words on divorce in Matthew 19:3-12. In this instance, the two divorce factions try to entrap Jesus by asking him whether divorce is permissible for any reason. Whichever way he answers, he will incur the wrath of one group or the other.

He reiterates his words from the Sermon: *No discarding of women as objects—period! No matter that Moses allowed for a certificate of divorcement!*

Later (Matthew 19: 10-12), after his adversaries have gone, the disciples press him on his answer. "If marriage is this unbreakable," they say, "it would be best never to marry!"

Jesus replies, "This is not for everyone—let him who can live by this teaching do so." Is this a loophole? Is Jesus giving some of us permission to divorce? *Not at all.* He is simply acknowledging the reality that we are all broken people and fall short of God's ideal intentions for us. When we do, there is forgiveness, and new life.

However, divorce is always a failure at best—a failure to live up to God's ideal for the human race.

Let me hasten to say here that I pastor a church where half of the adults have been divorced. They do not need lectures or scolding. Divorce is a grief experience. It is a "death."

We can hold high Jesus' ideal of monogamy for life and provide a community for healing and remarriage at the same time.

Most divorces are unnecessary. But when they occur, we must provide a family for broken families. At the same time, we must insist that vows before God are not to be taken lightly. I truly believe that God hates divorce. *I know the children who are victimized by it do!* Adults can say good-bye and trade for a newer model, but the children cannot. Husbands and wives can "split" and re-unite with new mates. The kids stay split *forever.*

I also know for certain that our civilization will implode without solid families. No one should be forced by law or sermon to remain in an abusive relationship. But by the same token, no one should ever doubt that marriage is God's sacred gift to a healthy society.

The Way, Beyond Oaths
(Matthew 5:33-37)

Oath-swearing these days is confined mainly to courts of law. And lying under oath—perjury—is a crime. However, in Jesus' time, oaths were used regularly in everyday life. One could *swear* by different objects: by *God*, by *earth*, by *heaven*, by *Jerusalem*, or even by one's own *head*.

Also, the objects by which one swore carried different degrees of punishment if the oaths were broken. For example, if you swore by God, you could not break your oath. But there was much debate as to whether other oaths could be broken.

In fact, truth-telling had been reduced to the point where it was okay to lie as long as one didn't lie under oath.

Does that sound familiar?

Again, Jesus takes the issue beyond what is legal to what is right. He says, don't swear by anything—by heaven, or earth, or Jerusalem, or your own head. When you are asked to testify, just say *yes* and *no*. Truth-telling has nothing to do with an official oath. It is a direct result of the wayfarer's relationship to God. Truth-telling is a *sacred* matter, not merely a *legal* one.

Jf there is any lesson we have
learned in Twentieth-Century
America, it is that truth-telling
has very little to do with swearing
to tell the truth. As the code
books have grown thicker, skirt-
ing the truth has grown craftier.

There is a maxim that says, the more laws a
society needs to enforce truth-telling, the less the
truth is being told.

Truth-telling is as vital to preserving society
and pointing to God as sexual fidelity is to family solidarity.

Some interpreters have taken this text as a pro-
hibition against swearing oaths in court or when
assuming public office. This misses Jesus' point.
He's saying that oath swearing is a mere formal-
ity. It's harmless. It does not guarantee truth-
telling. Every *yes* and every *no* uttered by a wayfarer is the same as a sacred oath because the wayfarer speaks for God. Adding the connotation of
the sacred to something that is already sacred is
superfluous.

The Way, Beyond Revenge (Matthew 5:38-42)

Probably no teaching of Jesus has been debated, argued, analyzed, and embellished more than this passage. It is subject to every interpretive abuse imaginable. Therefore, I shall try to examine what Jesus said, and not go chasing the rabbits of capital punishment, war, or other issues.

Of first importance is to remember that Jesus' speaking about *revenge* here is one of six illustrations of what it means to be *salt* (preserve society) and *light* (point beyond the law). It is not a full-blown treatise on law and order. It is a sermon illustration designed to give us a *right-brain* jolt.

"The Law says an eye for an eye and a tooth for a tooth." That's fair. The Jewish Law forbade taking a life for an eye or an arm for a tooth. Revenge had its limits. The idea was that it must be proportionate to the offense.

"But I say, *don't take revenge on someone who wrongs you.*" We usually stop here and start commenting. Let's read the rest of it. "If anyone slaps you on the right cheek, let him slap your left one too. If someone wins your shirt in a lawsuit, let

him have your coat too. And if one of the occupa-
tion troops forces you to carry his pack one mile,
carry it two. When someone begs you for a hand-
out, give it to him, and if he wants to borrow something, lend it to him."

The reason I insist on looking at Jesus' words
as one piece is because he's making one point by
using several vivid images.

The point is simply this: There is
only one way to stop the cycle of
revenge. Respond to it in contrast.
Someone must always leave the
last insult unanswered—the last
blow unreturned, the bully's de-
mands overmet, the beggar rewarded without insult, and the
debtor released.

This is not idealistic drivel. This is as real as
it gets! Violence travels in a deadly cycle. The
only way it ever gets broken is for someone to
recognize that the enemy is not another person,

but the *violence itself.*

Society must have laws to keep criminals at bay. Otherwise, all order would cease. But violence will never cease as long as punishment is the goal of incarceration. Someone has said, "If in order to defeat the beast, I become the beast, then bestiality wins."

Unfortunately, this principle has never been heeded on a wide scale. In fact, we have tended to silence those who espouse it.

At this writing, Yitzak Rabin, Prime Minister of Israel, is the latest victim. He dared pronounce that the "Palestinian question" could not be settled violently. Before that, it was Anwar Sadat of Egypt, slain by his own. And before that, Martin Luther King. And before that, Ghandi. And *Jesus.*

If we want to see a portrait of Satan, we mustn't look for horns and hooves. We only need look in the mirror at ourselves, whenever we become the beasts in order to defeat the beast.

My objection to the violence portrayed on television and in the cinema is not the graphic details themselves. I object to the two messages which these scenes
keep sending us: (1) that violence is good if the good
guys use it, and (2) that violence is the quickest and
easiest solution to all human conflicts.

I know this for certain. In those rare instances
when I have used Jesus' formula, on a personal basis, it
has worked beyond expectations.

The Way, Beyond Supremacism (Matthew 5:43-47)

Supremacism is our innate desire to be *better*
than someone else. It disguises itself as racism, pa-
rochialism, classism, and all of the other isms used
to separate people.

As the old southern white churchman put it:
"If I ain't better than a colored, black, African-
American or whatever you call him, who am I bet-
ter than?" Indeed!

For years, I missed this, the most monumental
of Jesus' illustrations of what wayfarers are supposed
to do when they're not in church. In the original
edition, I included this passage in the section on

revenge. I failed to see that Jesus was saving his most radical illustration for last.

His audience couldn't have been more dedicated to retaining their ethnic purity.

The kernel of all human evil is the refusal to see ourselves as the kinfolk of all fellow humans.

Jesus says, "You have been taught to love your own kind and exclude strangers. But I tell you to love strangers and pray for those who regard you as strangers. This is the only way that all of you can realize that you are the children of the Father in heaven. For God gives sun and rain to all without thinking in terms of 'good and bad'."

Interpretation: There's only one race. The human race.

Jesus says, "Why should you be rewarded if you love only those who love you? Nothing extraordinary about that. Even tax collector-traitors do *that!*"

Interpretation: The most distinguishing characteristic of the *followers of the way* is that they love people they don't know—not merely that they recognize the rights of all people—and not merely that they let others be. They love them as *family*.

Love, as Jesus used the word, has little to do with sentimentality but everything to do with good-will. It means to view others as equals.

What if we used these words as a searchlight and shined them upon modern *Christianity*? First, where would we aim the beam? At Catholics? At Protestants? At Mormons? At Evangelicals? There are too many *Christianities!* We have *compartmentalized* and *ethnicized* our own movement!

We must search for **wayfarers**, not *Christians*—that is, we must look for individuals from all of the *Christianities* who are on their way toward becoming like Jesus. They can be found in all places high and low, in different shapes and sizes. Their only distinguishing mark is that they love people unlike themselves because they recognize there are no people unlike themselves.

Summary: In the second section of the Sermon on the Mount, Jesus addresses how wayfarers are to relate to the everyday world. They are to go beyond what the law requires. They are to be like salt which preserves society. They are also to be guiding lights, which point people to a God of love.

What does this *salt/light* strategy entail? What are some examples of being salt and light? Here are six examples:

The Law says, don't murder. **Jesus says,** uproot the seeds of murder which are imbedded in your heart—unresolved anger, name-calling, sanctifying your cause by drafting God into your battles, and going to court as a first resort.

The Law says, don't commit adultery. **Jesus says,** don't let your sex drive lead you to treat others as objects. Sex is not a casual urge, but a sacred gift.

The Law says, if you divorce your wife, give her a legal certificate. **Jesus says,** don't casualize marriage.

The Law says, don't lie under oath. **Jesus says,** forget the oaths; just tell the truth.

The Law says, retaliate in kind when you've been wronged. **Jesus says,** respond in contrast. It's the only way to end the vicious cycle of violence.

The Law says, love your own kind and exclude strangers. **Jesus says,** there are no "they's," just "us's." There is nothing extraordinary about loving your own kind. You don't even need God to do that.

CHAPTER FOUR:

The Way
in the Soul

The Way in the Soul
(Matthew 6:1-18)

For God's Eyes Only
(Matthew 6:1)

Now that we know the wayfarer's role *out there* in the world, how are we to nourish our *inward selves*—our souls?

Jesus addresses this question in the third section of the Sermon by focusing on the three most prominent acts of Jewish devotion in his day: *almsgiving*, *prayer*, and *fasting*.

Just as there was a key verse in the second section of the Sermon, so there is a pivotal verse that governs this section:

81

Make sure that you avoid religious exhibitionism. If you start playing to the crowd, applause is all you will receive, and your heavenly father will not reward you within (Matthew 6:1).

This was another bombshell. His listeners thought that the two main purposes of these devotional acts were to *appease God* and to *impress onlookers.* Almsgiving, prayer, and fasting had become art forms designed to magnify the believer's sincerity and to merit God's favor.

And here comes Jesus saying religious devotion at its best is designed to enjoy God on the *secret soul-level.*

The key repetitive phrase in this passage is: "And the Father who sees what you do in secret—on the soul level—will reward you in secret."

Point: Whatever we do to strengthen our intimate bond with God should be kept intimate—sacredly private. For God's eyes only!

Just as there is physical modesty—we don't get naked in front of everyone—and just as there is psychological modesty—we don't bare our innermost thoughts to everyone—so there is a spiritual modesty. We don't expose our private communion with God.

We don't have to appease God. He already loves us. And, we have already been instructed on how to be salt and light to the world. Giving, praying, and fasting are not ways of exhibiting our piety to onlookers. They are ways of enjoying God on the soul level.

Giving as Self-Enrichment (Matthew 6:2-4)

If the purpose of giving is not to appease God or to impress others, what is it? Obviously, the main purpose is to help needy recipients in a private way that preserves their dignity. But there is another key purpose.

When generosity is kept private, the donor discovers that he enriches himself by giving. That's what Jesus means when he says repeatedly, "and the Father who sees your secret act will reward you in your secret self."

Giving is the best thing we can do for our

internal fitness. Of course, most people who read this immediately think it is simply another pious ploy to lift money off them.

All I can say is, "Don't knock it 'til you've tried it." *Nothing enriches my innards like giving anonymously.*

What about fundraisers, and name plaques, and memorials, and publicized philanthropy? Is Jesus negating these? Not at all. His emphasis is on *motive,* not *method.* The question is, why do we give? To draw praised attention? Or to enrich others?

Jesus didn't forbid public generosity. He told a rich man to "go-sell-give-come-follow." I assume the rich man's generosity would not have gone unnoticed. Jesus also watched as people filed by to make public donations to the temple. He applauded the poor widow who gave her livelihood, and chided the rich guy who gave leftovers.

Back to our focus. This section is about becoming spiritually fit on the *inside.* The soul that enjoys God discovers that giving becomes self-enrichment.

Praying as Self-Adjustment
(Matthew 6:5-15)

The purpose of prayer, like giving, is not to earn God's favor or change his mind. It is to change us to fit his will and mind. Prayer changes the person who prays—prayer is self-adjustment! Another bombshell.

"When you pray, don't do as the grandstanders who like to stand in the synagogues or on the streets," says Jesus. "They like to stop traffic with their bobbing and mumbling. Attention is what they are after, and I assure you that's all they get —people's attention! When you pray, go into your private room, shut the door, and pray secretly to your unseen Father. And your Father who hears your secret prayers will reward you" (Matthew 6:5-6).

When I observe modern prayers and listen to the philosophy of prayer which is modeled by religious leaders—alas, when I observe my own prayer life—I wonder if we've ever heard what Jesus is saying here.

A friend just lost his wife to cancer. She battled it twelve years. The last time she came out of remission, she decided not to take additional treatment. She and her husband and children made peace with her death.

A few days before she died, some "friends" visited her and announced that they knew of a woman who could cure her cancer with a special regimen of prayer and holistic diet—if only she and her family had the faith to pray "correctly."

How barbaric! *Religion is at its sickest when it suggests that overcoming terminal illness is a matter of technique in prayer!* It presupposes that God only listens to those who get their incantations right.

Thankfully, my friend's wife was able to employ prayer in its most powerful form—namely, to know the comfort and presence of God in her waning days. She didn't use prayer to get God to *change* her circumstance. She used it *to adjust herself* to fit her circumstance. Prayer does indeed change things. It changes things like *fear*, *panic*, and *hopelessness*.

Speaking of technique: How should we pray? What are the mechanics of prayer?

Jesus gives the simplest of answers to these question—but again, I wonder if we hear him?

"Don't use meaningless, repetitive words, and don't confuse length with effectiveness. This is what pagans do. They think length and mumbo jumbo can change God. Keep this in mind: Your Father in heaven already knows what you need before you ask him."

Praying is not an alarm clock whose purpose is to awaken God! It is an intimate visit with our loving Father—a secluded conversation with a happy parent.

"If you want a practical demon-stration," says Jesus, "then pray like this:
"Father in heaven, let your name be honored here on earth as in heaven. Let your Kingdom come and your will prevail in me. Give me what I need to survive: food for my body; mercy for my spirit; mercifulness for my relationships; and courage to withstand the evil one who resides in me."

I have taken liberty in rendering the Lord's Prayer because I don't believe Jesus intended for us to memorize it and repeat it verbatim. After all, he's just finished warning us away from repetitious and memorized praying. I don't view it as the Lord's prayer, but as a *sample* prayer.

I think Jesus was saying, "Use your own words to say something like this." The central themes of the sample prayer are more important than the words.

First, there is the recognition of God as both the awesome source of all things and our personal loving Father. Second, there is our willing surrender to his leadership. Third, there is the simple request that our basic needs be met—*physical, spiritual,* and *relational.*

Jesus now makes it clear that there is one final and vital element which overshadows all praying—namely, the spirit of forgiveness.

"No need to pray," he says, "unless you're willing to give the same mercy you are requesting from God" (Matthew 6:14-15).

J have examined Jesus' words on forgiveness from every angle. J have tried to find a loophole in the phrase: "Jf you do not forgive others, God will not forgive you." Jt cannot be translated otherwise and be faithfully translated! He means what he says.

This puts all of us in a corner. Rarely do we pray with no malice in our hearts. Is there a way around this harsh saying of Jesus? No. But there is a way through it. We can confess our inability to forgive.

We can say, "God, forgive me, I cannot forgive." This is not a gimmick for receiving God's forgiveness. It is a request for one of the basic needs of survival. Just as I need basics like food and shelter for survival, I need the *courage* and *grace* to *forgive*. It is something I don't have and cannot invent. It is a *gift*. Whenever I ask for the gift of forgiveness, the results are amazing.

Self-Denial as Self-Love (Matthew 6:16–18)

Jesus repeats the principle of secrecy when addressing the third prominent practice of Jewish devotion—*fasting*. "Don't put on a sad face when you fast. Hypocrites have to do this in order to be applauded. As I said before, applause is all they will ever receive. When you fast, don't let it show. Make sure only God knows, and you will receive your rewards from him."

Nowadays, it seems that either most of us follow Jesus' instructions on fasting, or few of us fast at all. We rarely hear of the practice anymore.

I don't know that there is any shame in this.

Before we decide, we need to know something of
the meaning of fasting in Jesus' day.

Fasting was an integral part of Jewish religious
life. The fast lasted from dawn to sunset, after which
normal meals could be eaten. Fasting was connected
to several occasions. People in *mourning* fasted during the time between the death and burial of loved
ones. Fasting was also an act of national mourning
or *penitence*. Sometimes, fasting was a preparation
for *revelation*. The key factor was that fasting in all
its forms was an exercise in self-denial designed to
gain the *attention* and *favor* of God.

Obviously, Jesus had another grenade to throw
at this kind of thinking. Fasting, like prayer, is not
to gain God's favor. Its purpose is to change the
one who fasts! Healthy self-denial in any form is an
act of self-love. Its purpose is to strengthen our
ability to govern our inward urges.

How are we to regard this ancient practice?
Should we fast? My own view is that we should
indeed find ways to place our appetite for God above
all of our other appetites. Spiritual need precedes
physical need. If we believe this, we should practice
it in a disciplined fashion.

To me, fasting is but one of several ways to put
God before our consumptive urges. It is one of

many examples of self-control. We all have the problem with defining when we've had enough—enough food, sex, money, toys, acclaim, or other things.

A regimen of self-deprivation for God's sake is healthy, and we should hear more about it from America's pulpits.

There is a great need in modern society to refute two prevalent lies about human nature. One says that denying our basic urges is damaging. The other says that self-indulgence is a civil right.

I rigorously object. In the first case, human beings would not have evolved to a civilized state if basic urges weren't governed and denied. In the second case, self-indulgence is not a civil right.

I do not have the right to feed my every whim. I am part of a community. Self-indulgence does not occur in a vacuum. If I abuse myself, I abuse you and vice-versa.

How long must we suffer the lies that enthrone moral anarchy under the guise of First Amendment rights?

Summary

The third section of the Sermon on the Mount (Matthew 6:1-18) addresses religious devotion, or the question of how wayfarers are to practice their inward relationship with God. Jesus answers the question with one overarching theme: Practice your piety in *secret*, so that God can mold you *within*.

Do not practice your piety for public attention. Your role is to love people in public and to give alms, pray, and fast in private.

Almsgiving, prayer, and fasting are designed to change the participants, not God or onlookers.

CHAPTER FIVE:

The Way and Wealth

The Way
and Wealth
(Matthew 5:13-48, 6:22-34)

Your God and Your Money
(Matthew 6:24)

In the fourth section of the Sermon, Jesus deals with what he evidently thinks is the most difficult issue facing followers of the way: namely, how to relate to and handle material wealth.

I say *evidently* because Jesus spoke about this subject more than almost any other. His parables and discourses were filled with references to *persons and their purses.*

95

As in the other sections of the Sermon, there is a key verse that states a basic principle. This principle in turn informs the rest of the section. Matthew 6:24 is the key verse here. "No one can serve two masters and be one slave. He will hate one and love the other or be loyal to one and disloyal to the other. You cannot serve both God and money."

In this verse, the word translated "money" is *mammon*. Some scholars think Jesus was referring to some god whom his listeners easily recognized, but they differ as to the origin of this pagan deity. Others say Jesus was simply personifying wealth for dramatic effect—as in, "You cannot serve both God and The Almighty Dollar!"

Either way, the point is the same. Jesus is recognizing that human nature has a way of deifying wealth.
In spite of all of our preachments to the contrary, we give wealth a sacred status.

I believe that this obsession with the accumulation and protection of wealth is really a symptom of our hunger for immortality. We are mortal creatures who can perceive immortality. We crave *security* or *freedom from want*. And when freedom from want is the driving force within, we have only three alternatives. We can follow the path of Eastern religion and aim at achieving a state of *cessation from wanting*. That is, we can see the quest for all things material as being evil in itself. The Hindu-Buddhist quest is to cease to exist in this material world by a series of transmigrations of the soul.

I was only about twenty the first time I asked a Buddhist monk if he wanted to be "saved." I was totally baffled when he said, "No! I want the wanting of my ego to die. I want to escape the evil of material being. I want for there to be nothing singularly identifiable left of me to save."

A second alternative in our quest for the freedom from want is the Western solution that is manifested most in American consumerism. The trite anecdote, "He who dies with the most toys wins!" is truer than we like to admit. The great migration from Europe to America was more about free land than free religion. The current outbreak of worldwide democracy is more about capitalist consumerism than political freedom.

This is not all bad. In fact, it is better than the Communist and Fascist alternatives. The freedom to earn, accumulate, and protect wealth plays to human self-interest. In a broken world, it is better than any other system humans have yet to devise.

Thankfully, however, consumerism is not the best alternative. There is another way besides hating wealth or worshipping wealth. It is *the way* taught and modeled by Jesus.

He did not see matter as evil in and of itself. God created matter; therefore it is good. Nor did he condemn the wealthy or equate goodness with poverty. It is a gross distortion to make Jesus the champion of any economic, political, or moral class. Read the New Testament! He hung out with *all* of them. He loved *all* of them. He favored none of them over the others.

What sets Jesus' way apart from
the anti-matter and pro-matter ide-
ologies is simply this:
He showed that spirit and matter
can live in harmony in one human
being.

The incarnation—God wrapped in human flesh—is about the joining of *matter* and *spirit*. It is God's declaration that he will redeem us— body, spirit, and all. Jesus' spirit, or soul, was not the only thing resurrected on Easter morning. He was resurrected both body and soul. He was a psychophysical unity.

I am not quibbling over philosophies here. This is crucial to the way we relate to wealth. Jesus gave us an alternative to the Eastern tendency to ignore poverty and to keep masses of people locked in the caste of their birth. And he also gave us an alternative to Western materialism that locks masses of people in the "race for toys." *Spirit* and *matter* can live in the same house.

How? Let's look again at the central verse:

You cannot serve both God and mammon—money personified (Matthew 6: 24). The key is to *love* persons and *use* money. Money is *not* a person. God *is* a person. People *are* persons. Money is an instrument, a tool. If we allow it to become personalized, we end up loving money and using persons.

And how do we keep from personifying and deifying money? Jesus answers by addressing our two biggest problems with money.

Winding up the Zeroes (Matthew 6:19-21)

One of our biggest problems with wealth, of course, is our *addiction to accumulating.* When I first wrote on this subject twenty years ago, I wrote from the perspective of a lower-middle income American. The resource books I used to interpret Jesus' words were all written by economic peers.

Then I had occasion to earn more money than I ever dreamed. Most of it was subsequently lost or given away. However, I now enjoy an income that is higher than I thought I would ever enjoy.

I share this merely to say that I now understand firsthand Jesus' caution about *winding up the zeroes.*

"Do not pile up riches on earth, where moths and rust destroy, and robbers break in and steal. Instead, pile up riches in heaven, where moths, rust, and thieves cannot destroy. For your heart will always be where your riches are" (Matthew 6:19-21).

This is not an *anti-savings* commandment! We need to be clear about that, up front. There is absolutely nothing wrong with accumulating wealth. On the contrary, wealth should be accumulated to be used properly. Jesus told more than one parable about God honoring those who multiply his gifts.

This is about *where we keep our hearts.* It is about who tells us who we are and where we place our ultimate trust.

Jesus is telling us that we cannot accumulate enough *stuff* to ever be at peace with our life, our death, and our future. We cannot get from money that which can come only from God—the power to calm all fear.

I learned this the hard way, as I mentioned earlier. A mere five years after writing essentially what I'm saying here, I was on the treadmill of deal making for the sake of deal making. I had the toys, but someone else always had more. I fell into the trap of allowing the zeroes to tell me who I was—to define my heart.

Of course, I lied to myself by giving first ten percent, then twenty, and finally fifty percent to Christian "causes." In truth, I was bribing my conscience. My heart, indeed, was in my pocketbook, just where Jesus said it would be.

The *heart*, as we've said elsewhere, was regarded as the *internal command post* of all human action, thought, and feeling—the subconscious—the seat of our *self-image*.

So, Jesus is saying, accumulate "riches in heaven" and your heart will no longer be the captive of the transient and the mortal. In other words, you won't wax and wane with your wealth.

But, what does it mean to pile up riches in heaven? Volumes have been written about this. I think it simply means: Expend your energies on things that *last* vs. things that *don't*.

There is only one way to avoid being sucked into the vortex of materialism. Use wealth to enjoy persons—God and others. If you're winding up the zeroes, wind them up for God and others.

Wait to Worry
(Matthew 6:25-34)

The second and probably the biggest problem we have regarding wealth is *worry*. No need to elaborate. You already know. Whether rich or poor or in-between. If we don't have it, we worry about getting it. If we have it, we worry about keeping it. *Worry* is another word for *fear*.

Jesus knew this, of course. He spent more time speaking to financial anxiety than anything else. He does not say, "Don't worry." To worry is human. We are the only creatures who know of cause and effect. We can anticipate disaster in the future. And that's what worry is about—the future—things that have yet to happen.

Jesus' policy regarding financial anxiety was, **wait to worry**. Wait until the proper time! In Matthew 6:25-34, he defines the four proper times to worry. This may sound a bit satirical, but think about it.

First, worry when it will feed and clothe you.

"Look at the birds," he says. "They don't plant and reap and store, but your Father feeds them. And look at the weeds. They don't weave and sew, but your Father adorns them with beautiful blooms. Don't you know that you are worth more than birds and blooms?"

Worry is directly related to *self-worth*. If we knew what we're worth to God, we wouldn't worry.

Second, worry when it will add quantity or quality to your life.

In other words, when it will make you grow one inch or live one second longer. By all accounts, *worry subtracts quality and quantity from life.* Jesus says, "Worry when you want to shorten and cheapen your life. Otherwise, *wait!*"

Third, worry when you really want to know how it feels to be a pagan.

The pagans in Jesus' time were not godless

people. They were religious people who had unde-
pendable gods. Their gods were deceptive, capri-
cious, and ill tempered. They were untrustworthy.

Jesus is putting his finger on the chief source of
human anxiety. We are afraid that God is not really there for us, or if he is, he can't be trusted to
take care of us. After all, this was the key to Adam
and Eve's breach with the Creator. They were sus-
picious of God's intentions toward them.

"When you want to know how a pagan feels,
worry!" says Jesus. "Otherwise, wait."

Finally, worry when you want tomorrow to be worse than it's already going to be.

"Do not worry about tomorrow. It will have
problems of its own. There's no need to add to the
troubles tomorrow will bring" (Matthew 6: 34).

Note the realism here. Jesus doesn't sing the
old song, "Everything's gonna be O.K.!" He says
the opposite. "Everything's not gonna be O.K. The
future will be fraught with hurts. You want to make
them *worse*? Worry about them today."

But, there is more here than *pop psychology* and *positive mental attitude* stuff. Jesus says there is only one thing we should **not** wait to worry about: ***"The Kingdom of God in you"*** (Matthew 6: 33).

In other words, whether God reigns *within*.

Summary

Jesus' philosophy on how we are to relate to our wealth is an alternative to Eastern anti-materialism and Western consumerism. We can make peace with our money and use it as a blessing, provided that we do not expect it to give us what only God can give us.

The two problems which plague us regarding our material possessions are *greed*—the will to accumulate—and *anxiety*—the fear of tomorrow. The cure for both problems is trusting God and entrusting our futures to God. Making God the Lord of *today* and *tomorrow* is the only means of harmonizing the spiritual and material parts of our nature.

CHAPTER SIX:

The Way
of the Middle

The Way
of the Middle
(Matthew 7:1-29)

The Little Path is the Middle Path
(Matthew 7:13-14)

The pivotal passage in the fifth and final section of the Sermon is Matthew 7:13-14. Jesus says, "Go through the narrow gate; for the way that leads to destruction is wide and easy to follow, and there are many who travel it. But the way that leads to life is narrow and hard to travel, and few follow it."

Traditionally, the *narrow way* has been regarded as synonymous with narrow-mindedness and self-denial—the stuff of which doctrinaire and sectarian religions is made.

When we read the seventh chapter of Matthew as one piece, we discover that this wasn't what Jesus had in mind at all.

The narrow way is that tightrope which hangs between made-up minds on the right and on the left.

Jesus stayed in hot water with liberal and conservative factions alike. He was taught by all and bought by none. He traveled the most radical path of all—that razor's edge between extremes.

He was the master bladerunner.

Pharisees, Sadducees, and zealots all paused from their bickering long enough to join forces and persuade the Romans to do him in.

In Texas, we have a saying: The middle of the road has a yellow stripe because it's good for nothing but cowards and dead varmints. Jesus' reply would be that the reason people in the middle are dead is because they are run over by those coming from both directions! They live in *no-man's-land*.

There is always plenty of company to be had when you occupy the left or the right. "Broad is the way and many there are who follow it."

But the wayfarer's territory is in that difficult middle between absolutes.

Jesus uses several illustrations to describe what it means for wayfarers to steer the narrow middle course.

Between Judging and Condoning (Matthew 7:1-6)

In verses 1-5, we are warned away from *condemning* or *judging* others; but in verse 6, we are told not to give what is *holy* to dogs or throw our *pearls* in front of pigs.

"Do not judge others, so that you won't be judged by God. He will use your methods of judging others to judge you" (Matthew 7: 1-2). Now comes the *log* and *speck* analogy. "Remove the speck from your own eye before you start condemning the log in your brother's eye" (Matthew 7: 3-5).

So, we are not to condemn others. Condemning others is the flipside of forgiving others that he taught earlier. Just as God *forgives* us in proportion to our *forgiving*, so God *judges* us in proportion to our *judging*.

Jesus' detractors attacked him viciously at this point. He repeatedly associated with despicable characters without judging them. His refusal to condemn them was seen as an endorsement. There was no middle ground in the minds of his critics. Either you *condemned* or you *condoned*. And failing to condemn was tantamount to condoning.

They were probably so upset with his nonjudgmental lifestyle that they never heard him add, "Don't give what is holy to dogs; they will only turn and attack you. Do not throw your pearls in front of swine; they will only trample them underfoot." By this he meant that we do not have to surrender our moral convictions in the process of being nonjudgmental.

What are we to make of this? Is he saying, "Love the sinner, but hate the sin?" I don't think so. If that were his message, he would have come right out and said so. Besides, that posture is the easiest way I know to excuse ourselves from loving people who are unlike us in custom and habit.

I love you, but I hate your ways. Think of that for a moment. Would you be drawn to someone who said that to you? The message I get when I hear this is *you're not okay and I am*. It makes me want to defend my ways, even if I know my accuser is correct! It also makes me want to counterattack.

I think Jesus was trying to show us just how *narrow* the narrow way between condemning and condoning *is*! We are called to walk the *tight-rope*—to withhold our judgement of the behavior of others and to focus on our own. At the same time, we are to let God tell us what is holy and not throw away the goodness he has put in us. Herein lies the key: Whatever goodness or morality we have is not our doing. All *morality—all human goodness*—is derived from God. We don't come by it naturally.

The Way is narrow. It's that thin line between condoning and condemning.

The wayfarers' task is to keep silent and let others see the pearls of goodness God has given them. Throwing lectures and lessons at those who don't understand them is a waste of time, and it is counterproductive.

Between Desire and Realization (Matthew 7:7-11)

Jesus' second illustration of living in the middle deals with asking and receiving from God. In verses 7-8 he says, "Ask and you shall receive. Seek and you shall find. Knock and the door will be opened to you. For everyone who asks will receive and anyone who seeks will find, and the door will be opened to him who knocks."

All of the verbs in this passage are in the future tense. Jesus is not promising immediate fulfillment of our every desire. We must live by the agony of faith. We must walk mostly in darkness, daring to move forward on the basis of occasional glimpses of light on the far horizon.

As we said earlier, religion gets sick whenever it resorts to magic and promises the immediate realization of every desire.

I must also remind you of what we said about the biblical concept of the Kingdom of God in the opening chapter.

It has always been.
It is now growing.
But its fulfillment is yet to come.

Wayfarers must live between the
times. The way of the middle is
not for those who are steeped in
immediacy.

The courage to walk the narrow way between desire and realization, between certainty and doubt, comes from knowing the Father as Jesus did. "Would any of you fathers," he says, "give your son a stone if he asked for bread? As broken and imperfect as you are, you know how to give good gifts to your children. How much more, then, will your heavenly Father give good gifts to those who ask him!"

This raises the key question: What can we expect from God? All that we desire? Not at all. But we can expect good gifts—those gifts which are good for us. And the truth is, we don't know what's good for us. Only God knows. The issue is whether we can trust him while we live between desire and realization.

Between Loving and Being Loved (Matthew 7:12)

If wayfarers must live between desiring and realizing what they want from God, it follows that they must do the same thing with other people. This is the central meaning of what we call the Golden Rule. Literally the verse reads, "Whatever it is you want people to do to you, do it to them."

What do we want from others?
Love, fairness, acceptance, honesty, help, esteem, praise.
That pretty much covers it.
Well, that is what we are to give them, says Jesus.

"In a perfect world..." Of course, this one isn't; which is precisely Jesus' point. We cannot receive fully what we want and need from others. One of the great illusions is that another human being can fulfill all of our love needs. The result is an equal disillusionment. God alone knows the number of marriages that have been broken by the unrealistic expectation that a mate can completely fill one's emptiness.

Wayfarers are called to practice the Golden Rule anyway. We are to give our imperfect love and receive imperfect love. We must not lose heart just because others do. We have an advantage; we can love others because God loves us.

Between Doing and Believing (Matthew 7:15-27)

Jesus finishes the Sermon by illustrating the tension between *faith* and *works*—between being right with God by *believing* (trusting his way as truth) or by *doing*. Do we experience the Kingdom by doing right, or by being in a relationship built on trust?

As with the illustration on condemning vs. condoning, Jesus doesn't give us an outright answer. He leaves us in the *middle ground* of *both/and*. In verses

15-20, he says we can recognize false prophets by what they do. But in verses 22-23, he says that come Judgement Day, many miracle workers—doers—will be rejected because "I never knew you..."—because there was no relationship built on trust.

Doing good things for God without having a loving relationship with him is useless, and vice-versa. This point is driven home vividly in the parable of the two house builders, which concludes the Sermon (Matthew 7:24-27). The one who hears—*trusts Jesus' way*—but doesn't obey—*practices his beliefs*—is like a fool who builds his house in a dry riverbed. All that is needed to wash it away is one good storm.

On the other hand, the one who *hears—trusts Jesus' way*—and obeys—*does*—is like the wise man who built his house on a rock. It withstands all the storms.

I once attended a funeral service for a man who had been a known figure of the underworld. He had been convicted for murder, trafficking in drugs, and running a prostitution ring. The minister said, "Now we all know that Gus had his ups and downs, but I believe that he is in heaven at this very moment. For at the tender age of nine he accepted Jesus as his Lord and Savior during a vacation Bible school in this very church. No matter what he did later in life, his soul was secured in heaven from the moment he believed."

Perhaps Gus is in heaven—how would I know? I'm not God, and such matters are his business.

Perhaps the minister needed to say what he did in order to give hope and comfort to Gus's family. I too believe that we should always sound a note of hope. But I do not accept that Gus entered the Kingdom because he gave mental assent to a given number of truths at one time and in one place. We cannot get into the Kingdom merely because our theological head is screwed on straight! The Bible says that *even the devils* are quite orthodox (James 2:19).

On the other hand, there are some that would prefer to reduce discipleship to doing. What one *believes* doesn't matter; it's what he *does* that counts. I disagree.

What we believe about God, man, the world, and salvation is as important as what we do. For what we do will be determined by what we believe, just as what we believe will be proven by what we do.

The easy way—the way that is wide and broad and which leads to destruction—is the way of doing without believing or believing without doing. But the *narrow way* which leads to *life* is the middle way of *doing* and *believing*.

Summary

The narrow way that leads to life is the way of the tightrope. It is that razor's edge between extremes.

Few walk it.

Wayfarers must walk between condemning and condoning others. They must live between desiring and realizing God's promises. They must give love even when they don't receive it from other people, because they have received it from God. They are called to walk between faith and work, embracing both at the same time.

This is **Jesus, B.C.**

Kierkegaard was almost right when he said, "The Christianity of the New Testament simply does not exist. Instead, millions of people through the centuries have cunningly sought little by little to cheat God out of Christianity, and have succeeded in making Christianity exactly the opposite of what it is in the New Testament." [1]

He was incorrect only because he used the word, *Christianity*. What is in the New Testament is **The Way**. It preceded Christianity, and we've yet to follow it.

---

[1] Soren Kierkegaard, **Attack on Christendom**, trans. Walter Lowrie (Princeton, New Jersey: Princeton University Press, 1944), pp 32-33

About the Author

Dr. Gerald Mann is a minister, writer, humorist, businessman, and well-known voice for common sense Christianity. A native of West Columbia, Texas, Dr. Mann graduated from the University of Corpus Christi and earned a Master of Divinity (M.Div.) and a Doctor of Theology (Th.D.) from Southwestern Baptist Theological Seminary.

Dr. Mann has been featured in *TVGuide, USA Today, Advertising Age,* and *Texas Monthly.* He has been quoted by "NBC Nightly News," Paul Harvey, and nearly every major newspaper in America, including *US News and World Report,* and *The Wall Street Journal.*

Currently, his national television program, "Real Life...with Dr. Gerald Mann!," is available every Sunday in more than eighty million homes across America. He is chaplain of the Texas legislature and the pastor of Riverbend Church in Austin, Texas. Dr. Mann founded this church in 1979 with 60 adult family members. Today over 8,000 people regularly attend. He is the author of six books.

Dr. Mann married his high school sweetheart, Lois. They have three children.

For information regarding other books and tapes by Dr. Mann, call (512) 347-8608.